WHAT'S INSIDE

In this book, you will find the following chapters:

- Chapter 1: Letter from the Editor: Laura Little, Founder, and Chief Marketing Officer
- Chapter 2: The 3-Month Plan
- Chapter 3: Helpful Definitions
- Chapter 4: Recommended Learning Tools and Resources
- Chapter 5: Worksheets

Each chapter is broken down into sections, making it easy to understand and learn quickly.

CHAPTER 1

LETTER FROM THE EDITOR

Laura Little, founder and CMO

You can work in social media marketing if you choose to. Social media marketing is an excellent career choice. Almost every business globally has a social media presence, so your skills will always be in demand! Social media marketing is a perfect choice if you'd like to earn additional income outside of your "day" job or work full time in this career. Many people have turned freelance social media management into successful income-earning businesses or long-term careers.

I CREATED THIS GUIDEBOOK TO HELP YOU GET TO WHERE YOU NEED TO GO FAST AND WITHOUT THE FLUFF THAT SO MANY "GURUS" AND COURSES HAVE.

What are the most frequently asked questions on working in social media?

The most frequently asked questions about this topic are:

1. How do I get a job in social media?
2. What are the skills needed for a social media job?

3. What is the salary range for social media jobs?
4. What are the pros and cons of working in social media?
5. How to manage mental health in social media jobs.
6. Do you need a degree to work in social media management?

Lightening answer round!

How do I get a job in social media?
Learn a skill you can apply to the industry or profession of social media marketing.

What are the skills needed for a social media job?
The most common are graphic design, copywriting, and video creation.

What is the salary range for social media jobs?
It depends on where you live, but you can expect a minimum of $20–$25 per hour.

What are the pros and cons of working in social media?
The pros are that you can work from anywhere, and being surrounded by the latest technology and trends is fun. Cons are that it's high pressure, repetitive, and burnout can happen quickly.

How to manage mental health in social media jobs
Take breaks. Set boundaries.

Do you need a degree to work in social media management?
The answer is no! You'll need determination, practice, experience, and an understanding of the tools and techniques, but a degree is unnecessary.

CHAPTER 2

The 3-Month Plan

MONTH 1: PICK A LANE (FOR NOW) It can be overwhelming to understand the different areas of social media marketing, so I suggest starting with one or two categories and expanding as needed. Below are the potential categories for learning social media management; however, It's important to note that some companies require expertise in all areas, while others don't.

Here are some of your potential lanes:

- Creative- related to graphic design, copywriting, video, and visual content
- Strategy: related to planning, scheduling, and ideation
- Community - related to building relationships and groupmanagement.
- Data - related to understanding analytics and presenting metrics.
- Paid media - related to media buying and paying for advertising services.

I want to give you an example of knowing which lane might represent you best. For instance, if your brain is math-oriented and structure-oriented, you may prefer heading into the analytical parts of social media marketing. If you enjoy storytelling and visual content, you should explore more creative areas.

CHIEF MARKETING OFFICER TIP

Pick one area at a time and get training directly from the sources or software that you will use.

I've outlined the platforms that I think are worth exploring first. These platform recommendations are based on my personal experience using them and my knowledge of their current business and growth potential.

Although you might want to jump into learning, it's a bright idea to consider the below first.

Pick a lane and a platform that will keep you inspired and hired well into the future!

PLATFORMS RANKED

#1. Google/Alphabet Inc.

I have included Google as the number one platform on this list, even though the brand is not usually referred to as a social media platform. In my professional opinion, I think Google is the most significant player in the digital marketing industry. E-commerce brands rely on its search marketing capabilities, and Google search is deeply integrated with SEO and YouTube. Currently, 77% of internet users in the US aged 15-25 watch YouTube. (Bard, 2023) Additionally, Google is heavily invested in AI and virtual technology, which suggests that it will continue to introduce new advertising options and expand. This expansion could lead to more opportunities for you.

#2. X (formerly known as Twitter)

Twitter often receives criticism due to its owner, Elon Musk, but his ambitious vision for the future is undeniable. It is in Musk's best interest to make Twitter profitable and successful. Twitter was the first platform to introduce paid subscriber verification, demonstrating Musk's innovative approach. As a result, Twitter will remain a valuable platform to learn and utilize. Those who are early adopters who understand Twitter will have an advantageous skill set.

#3. Pinterest

Pinterest, for me, is the underdog that could. Pinterest is made for planners and seekers and carries many of the same components as a search engine. It has shown strong user growth, and as it has a relatively low number of digital marketing providers offering Pinterest-only services, it is number 3 on my list. Pinterest has had an 11% compound annual growth rate (CAGR) in the last three years. And in 2022, it is estimated to reach 465 million MAUs. (Bard, 2023)

#4. LinkedIn

LinkedIn is a business networking platform designed for professionals. While it may not fit the traditional definition of "social media," it offers many similar features, such as the ability to post, share, and build an audience. LinkedIn's parent company is Microsoft, which adds to its stability.

As of 2022, LinkedIn has over 830 million members and has generated revenue of $13.8 billion, indicating a promising future for the platform. (Bard, 2023)

#5. TikTok/ByteDance

ByteDance owns TikTok, a popular social media platform that features trending videos and dance-offs. One of the benefits of TikTok is its massive user base, with over 1 billion monthly active users worldwide as of January 2023. The United States is TikTok's biggest market, with over 100 million MAUs. However, there is a potential downside to using TikTok due to political relations with China. Although it is unlikely, there is still a risk that the US government could shut the app down at any time.

#6. Facebook, Instagram (Meta)

Probably the most famous of them all, I put Facebook and Instagram lower on the list as it's not convincing the versions of these platforms "as we know them now" will withstand the next decade. However, they are the most "known" and easy-to-enter platforms currently. Every business has a Facebook and Instagram account.

As of publication, "Threads" is the newest addition to the Meta umbrella; however, it's too early to tell if it will be successful or worth integrating into your career or business strategy.

My second reason for putting Meta at the bottom of the list as your first learning stop is that the provider market is highly saturated with freelance providers.

Some platforms didn't make my list, but that doesn't mean they aren't worth exploring.

Here are a few more to consider:

- Reddit
- Snapchat
- Quora
- Nextdoor
- Discord
- Twitch

Ultimately, you want to be *hired and inspired!* Like picking stocks, you want to play the long game, not the short one.

Refer to the helpful definitions chapter for deeper meanings and a

better understanding of expertise categories.

MONTH 2: GAIN SOME SOCIAL MEDIA MARKETING SKILLS!

A common misconception is that because a person might "use" social media, it means that they are automatically good at it!

I liken this thought process to owning a car. I drive and use my car, but I am not a mechanic. Using social media services and being a social media marketing professional are different.

As a social media manager, you'll need to have mastery of the platform you choose and understand the professional language used in the industry you choose.

EG: If you choose to focus on Pinterest, Do you know the fundamentals of Pinterest use?

Below, I've listed the five best learning websites for free learning directly from the biggest social media platforms. All offer certificates that could be used to win a job or build your freelance client base.

When you learn directly from the source, you'll be a part of their education system, and it's in the platform's best interest that you do well.

Meta Blue Print (Facebook & Instagram)
Canva Design School
TikTok Academy
Pinterest Academy
Google Skill Shop
LinkedIn Learning
Twitter / X

MONTH 3: GET SOCIAL MEDIA MARKETING EXPERIENCE
Once you've taken some classes and earned certificates of completion, it's time to get experience. Experience is more important than anything when winning new business, getting hired, or building a resume!

I understand that gaining experience without prior experience can be challenging, but it is possible. I know it's achievable because I have accomplished it myself. I don't have a formal marketing degree, and I got my first client by simply pitching my ideas.

When considering your strategy for gaining experience, you may need to take a *hit for the team* to start. What I mean by this is sometimes a compromise is involved *now* to get ahead later.

That compromise could be time, it could be money, and it will undoubtedly be effort, but remember, you are thinking about the long game, not the short game.

Here are three proven ways to gain the experience necessary to start a career or business in social media marketing.

INTERNSHIPS are fantastic because the company knows you are there to learn, and often, they will hire from within, which means you could be up for the next opportunity that opens. Look for digital marketing agencies or startups that offer internships, as they can provide valuable hands-on experience and mentorship.

Even if the training is unpaid, the experience and networking opportunities can be highly beneficial for your career in digital marketing.

VOLUNTEER to help a local organization or non-profit for free. Many non-profit organizations use digital marketing to promote their causes and reach their target audience. Offer your services as a digital marketing volunteer. Not only will you gain practical experience, but you'll also be contributing to a meaningful cause, and you can ask for a testimonial or reference.

CREATE a professional project that you can use to display your expertise. For example, if you love cooking, create a Social Media Account related to cooking. Use it as a calling card to show off your community or graphic design skills.

CHIEF MARKETING OFFICER TIP:
Get strategic about how you work towards getting experience.
If you love and want to work in the beauty industry, don't volunteer to do social media marketing for a local restaurant.

Focusing on one industry can be helpful to set yourself up for being hired in that category.

Should I work for free?
Generally, I do not advocate working for free because time is money, and we all need to live. However, when you have a gratis/ free **strategy** that is transactionally helpful TO YOU, then I highly encourage it.

GRATIS / FREE STRATEGIES
So, what exactly is a gratis/free strategy?

A gratis/free strategy is a plan that you make to help you get hired in the niche and industry that you want to be in.

It could be a service that you provide in exchange for a testimonial or review.

Being strategic is the key to building your portfolio quickly and getting hired fast.

Here's an example

You want to work with **Graphic Design** for Social Media
You want to focus on **Pinterest** as your platform
You need to showcase **Vertical Design** skills in the format of video and static images.

<u>Your strategic offer</u>: I will design five vertical pins and two vertical pins with video for your brand *gratis* in *exchange* for a testimonial on the quality of my service.

<u>CHIEF MARKETING OFFICER TIP</u>
Keep these offerings small and highly focused on where you want to show your expertise.

MONTH 4: BUILD YOUR RESUME AND PORTFOLIO
Before you go out and pitch yourself to paying clients or potential hiring companies, you must put your best foot forward by showcasing your experience and skills.

The quickest way to do this is by using a LinkedIn profile. It's faster than building a website. It's 100% free and functions perfectly for everything you need to do to win a job or get new business. With a well-formulated LinkedIn profile, you can

- List your expertise
- Present your credentials
- Show off your work experience

- Connect with hiring managers
- Display your portfolio
- Create and share content that highlights who you are and raises your visibility.
- Ask for testimonials and reviews
- Join professional groups related to digital marketing.

I love LinkedIn as a jumping-off point because it's incredibly user-friendly, fast to set up, and free!

While creating a website might be one of the first things that comes to mind to market yourself, I advise against this initially. Go with the most straightforward, most accessible thing. PLUS, LinkedIn is a massive professional search engine, so you'll already be where the right people are looking!

If you want more support in creating a fantastic LinkedIn profile, I recommend you follow LinkedIn expert Mandy McEwen. She shares her expertise in LinkedIn profile creation and using and leveraging LinkedIn for business. She is also on YouTube!

Link: https://www.LinkedIn.com/in/mandymcewen

CHIEF MARKETING OFFICER LinkedIn TIP

- Fill out your profile completely.
- Add a professional photo.
- Add all your skills.
- Ask for testimonials!

MONTH 5. SOURCE OPPORTUNITIES!

The process is the same whether you are looking for a full-time job or kicking off your freelance career. Find the opportunity, pitch it, and win it!

Head to the resources and recommended tools chapter for a list of sites that feature Social Media Marketing Jobs.

LET'S TALK MONEY

WHAT IS THE SALARY RANGE FOR A SOCIAL MEDIA MANAGER?

The salary range of a full-time Social Media Manager is like anything, variable. Your salary will depend on experience, skills, location, and type of company/company size.

Companies like Glassdoor.com can help you understand an expected or average salary range.

CHIEF MARKETING OFFICER TIP

Research a company thoroughly before you apply. Is the company transparent? Do they have a culture that suits your expectations and lifestyle? Do they have proof of concept? How long have they been in business? Doing a bit of research prior can save you from career drama in the future.

I've listed three entry-level social media manager salaried positions with salary ranges for reference. I do not know any of these brands. I simply did a quick LinkedIn search.

Title: Social Media Manager
Brand: Signature Solar
Location: Texas:
Onsite: $50k Per year + Benefits

Title: Social Media Manager
Brand: Creative Circle
Location: Florida
Hybrid: $35-$45 per hour

Title: Social Media Manager
Brand: Stanford University
Location: Stanford
Onsite: $99k

WHAT IS THE SALARY RANGE FOR A *FREELANCE* SOCIAL MEDIA MANAGER?

Freelance project rates vary based on company, project scope, company size, and industry.

CHAPTER 3

HELPFUL MARKETING AND
CAREER DEFINITIONS

ORGANIC SOCIAL MEDIA MARKETING: Organic social media marketing refers to the process of promoting and marketing a brand, product, or service on social media platforms through non-paid methods. It involves creating and sharing relevant, engaging, and valuable ***content** to attract and engage with the target audience, build brand awareness, foster customer relationships, and drive organic traffic to a website or social media profile.

*See the definition of Digital Marketing Content

PAID SOCIAL MEDIA MARKETING: Paid social media marketing refers to advertising and sponsored content on social media platforms to reach a specific target audience. It involves allocating a budget to create and run paid campaigns, such as display ads, promoted posts, or sponsored content, to increase brand visibility, reach a wider audience, drive traffic, and generate leads or conversions.

DIGITAL MARKETING CONTENT: Digital marketing content refers to any type of media or information that is created, curated, and shared online to promote a brand, product, or service. It includes various formats such as blog posts, articles, videos, images, infographics, podcasts, webinars, social media posts, and more.

If you have a passion for writing or visual art, digital marketing content creation may be an area to explore.

DIGITAL MARKETING ANALYTICS: Digital marketing analytics involves the collection, measurement, analysis, and interpretation of data related to digital marketing efforts. It encompasses tracking and analyzing various metrics, such as website traffic, engagement rates, conversion rates, click-through rates, social media metrics, customer behavior, and more. The insights gained from digital marketing analytics help marketers make informed decisions, optimize campaigns, identify trends, and measure the effectiveness of their marketing strategies.

BRAND IDENTITY: Brand identity refers to the visual and verbal elements that distinguish a brand and help create a unique and recognizable image in the minds of consumers. It encompasses the brand's logo, colors, typography, tagline, voice, tone, and overall personality.

Brand identity plays a crucial role in establishing a brand's reputation, conveying its values and attributes, and building a solid connection with the target audience.

DIGITAL MARKETING STRATEGY: A digital marketing strategy is a comprehensive plan that outlines the goals, tactics, and channels used in promoting a brand, product, or service online.

SEARCH ENGINE OPTIMIZATION (SEO): Search Engine Optimization (SEO) is the practice of optimizing a website or online content to improve its visibility and ranking on search engine results pages (SERPs).

SOCIAL MEDIA ENGAGEMENT: Social media engagement refers to the interaction, involvement, and responsiveness of users with social media content and profiles. It encompasses actions such as likes, comments, shares, retweets, mentions, direct messages, and clicks. Social media engagement is an essential metric for measuring the effectiveness of social media marketing efforts and indicates the level of audience interest, brand affinity, and the potential for viral reach.

*Please note that these definitions are general and may vary depending on specific contexts and interpretations within the field of digital marketing.

SOCIAL MEDIA MARKETING MANAGER: Responsible for developing and executing social media marketing strategies to achieve business goals. The roles could include creating and managing social media content, running ads, and measuring social media results.

SOCIAL MEDIA STRATEGIST: Develops the overall social media strategy for a company or brand. This includes identifying target audiences, setting goals, and developing content and social media campaigns.

SOCIAL MEDIA COMMUNITY MANAGER: Responsible for building and maintaining a positive and engaged community around a brand or organization on social media. They do this by creating and sharing content, responding to comments and questions, and resolving issues.

CHAPTER 4

One way to improve your chances of finding social media marketing jobs is to explore full-time and freelance options.

To get started, look at this list of websites where you can find relevant job postings. With a little effort and persistence, you can land a job that's the right fit for your skills and interests!

- Upwork (www.upwork.com)
- Freelancer (www.freelancer.com)
- Fiverr (www.fiverr.com)
- Guru (www.guru.com)
- Toptal (www.toptal.com)
- PeoplePerHour (www.peopleperhour.com)
- Simply Hired (www.simplyhired.com)
- FlexJobs (www.flexjobs.com)
- Freelanced (www.freelanced.com)
- 99designs (www.99designs.com)
- Behance (www.behance.net)
- Dribbble (www.dribbble.com)
- LinkedIn ProFinder (www.LinkedIn.com/profinder)
- Remote OK (www.remoteok.io)
- We Work Remotely (www.weworkremotely.com)

- AngelList (www.angel.co)
- Workana (www.workana.com)
- Digital Marketing Jobs (www.digitalmarketingjobs.com)
- Indeed (www.indeed.com)
- Glassdoor (www.glassdoor.com)
- Monster (www.monster.com)
- The Creative Group (www.roberthalf.com/the-creative-group)
- Mediabistro (www.mediabistro.com)
- Craigslist (www.craigslist.org)
- Authentic Jobs (www.authenticjobs.com)
- Krop (www.krop.com)
- Smashing Jobs (www.smashingjobs.com)
- Remote.co (www.remote.co)
- Dice (www.dice.com)
- Dynamite Jobs (https://dynamitejobs.com/)
- Working Nomads (https://www.workingnomads.com)
- iHire Marketing (https://www.ihiremarketing.com/)
- Freelance Digital Marketing Jobs Facebook groups (e.g., "Digital Marketing Freelancers")
- Social Media, Marketing & PR Jobs (ww.facebook.com/groups/socialmediajobs)

A NOTE ON MENTAL HEALTH

It would be unfair of me to not talk a little bit about Mental Health as it relates to Social Media Marketing and Digital Marketing.

I have found this career path exciting and rewarding, but I also, at times, have felt burned out and exhausted.

Social Media Managers and digital marketing professionals, over time can experience a below-average quality of Mental Health because of their exposure to Social Media.

- A study by the University of West Virginia found that social media managers have a lower mental health score than the general population. The average mental health score for social media managers was 6.35 out of 10, while the average mental health score for the general population was 7.12. (Bard, 2023)

- The study also found that social media managers are more

likely to experience symptoms of anxiety and depression than the general population. (Bard, 2023)

- 40% of social media managers reported experiencing symptoms of anxiety, while 33% reported experiencing symptoms of depression.
- The study's authors believe that the high levels of stress and burnout experienced by social media managers are to blame for their lower mental health scores. Social media managers are constantly bombarded with negative comments and feedback, and they are often required to work long hours and meet unrealistic expectations.

Factors that can contribute to this experience include,

- Exposure to harmful content: Social media users are often exposed to damaging content, such as cyberbullying, trolling, and hate speech. This can be a significant source of stress and anxiety for social media managers responsible for monitoring and responding to this content.
- Excessive comparison to others: Social media can be a breeding ground for comparison. Social media users are constantly bombarded with images and videos of people who seem to be happier, more successful, and more attractive than themselves. This can lead to feelings of inadequacy and low self-esteem.
- Work-life balance: Social media managers often have to work long hours and be available 24/7. This can make it challenging to maintain a healthy work-life balance.

This experience can be mitigated by

- Setting boundaries,
- Taking breaks,
- Practicing self-care.

I hope you've found this book a valuable resource!

Good luck on your journey to Social Media Marketing Mastery and finding your perfect job!

CHAPTER 5

Worksheets to help you plan!

My strategy (fill in the blanks)

I want to work with __________ in Social Media Marketing
I want to focus on __________as my platform
I need to showcase __________ skills in the format of __________

<u>My strategic offer</u>: I will (skill) __________ amount __________ of __________ for a company in ______ *gratis* in *exchange* for a testimonial on the quality of my service.

My strategy (fill in the blanks)

I want to work with __________ in Social Media Marketing
I want to focus on __________as my platform
I need to showcase __________ skills in the format of __________

<u>My strategic offer</u>: I will (skill) __________ amount __________ of __________ for a company in ______ *gratis* in *exchange* for a testimonial on the quality of my service.

ABOUT THE EDITOR / AUTHOR

LAURA LITTLE is a talented marketing professional and Fractional Chief Marketing officer. With over ten years of experience in business development, business marketing, and strategy.

She is the founder of "That British Chick" Digital Marketing Company, which helps startups, founders, and brands with creative ideas and strategies in Digital Marketing. In 2020, she founded the Females In Digital Marketing platform an online collective supporting over 15,000 women globally through educational online courses, books, workshops, jobs, and community.

In 2024 she re-branded Females In Digital Marketing to X Factr Coaching. You can find information on business coaching and Laura Little using the links below.

Agency: www.thatbritishchick.com
LinkedIn: www.LinkedIn.com/in/lauralittlenyc/